RETIRED

in Williamsburg

• • •

BY FREDERICK

ISBN: 1451590482
ISBN-13: 9781451590487

Library of Congress Control Number: 2010904848

Retired in Williamsburg

FORWARD

To be a cartoonist is hard enough. To be an editorial cartoonist is madness. When done properly, it combines artistry with extraordinary wit. Fred Siegel has succeeded with "Retired in Williamsburg" because he brings the irony of local and national news to a human level of bemusement. He captures the heart of the conversation in simple sentences that someone else's blog would take reams to convey. Any retired fellow, or anyone else for that matter, can identify with the contradictions posed and feel like replying in kind. Fred could just as well call his venture "Wish I'd Said That."

- Bill O'Donovan, March 30, 2010
Publisher, "The Virginia Gazette"

ACKNOWLEDGEMENTS

When we decided to retire, we developed a wish list of requirements for our retirement location. The list included some obvious items like; one home, four seasons, close to the ocean, a college presence, good health care and airport access. We then started to visit the usual suspects along the Atlantic coast from Annapolis to Savannah. While there are some clever communities in this geography, it became clear that Williamsburg was the best location. After nine years, we know that we made the correct retirement choice. It has met our above wish list and has the powerful combination Colonial Williamsburg's Restored area and the College of William & Mary.

I started to think of how I could relate the story of this wonderful retiree experience in Williamsburg to friends and neighbors, and to those people who might have an interest in moving here. I developed the idea of two people walking past buildings in the restored area while commenting on retiree experiences and giving opinions on local, Virginia and national politics. I drew pictures of seven historic buildings and started to add commentary to the drawings.

In December of 2007 I approached Bill O'Donovan, Publisher of the Virginia Gazette, with the "Retired in Williamsburg" cartoon idea. I thank him for his support and willingness to launch the concept on the Editorial Page in the Saturday edition. With some great ideas about content from Rusty Carter, Editor, the cartoon was first published on February 2, 2008. I had wonderful guidance from the best newspaper Copy Editor in the Commonwealth, Robbie Steele. Robbie has the great ability of converting my ideas from lengthy sentences into words that tell the story and still fit in the balloons of the cartoon.

Finally, I want to thank my wife, Barbie, who for 45 years has been my biggest supporter during my business career and now as her retired husband. In this cartoon adventure, Barbie has been my corporate conscience, making sure I stay within generally accepted guidelines, which is getting tougher as I get older. I hope you enjoy reading the cartoons as much as I enjoyed creating them.

DEDICATION

This book is dedicated to the Board Members, Staff and Volunteers of the Hospice House of Williamsburg. They are very important caregivers to the members of our community. It was here that one of my best friends, Harvey Johnson, spent his last precious days.

CHAPTER
1

. . .

Life as a Retiree

Barbie: I hope we are not late for the "Tea Party" meeting in Washington.

Fred: No problem, we will take the Toyota.

Bob: You look like you just had a 'moment of truth' experience.

Ray: You're right. This morning when I was in the middle of a heated argument with my wife, I realized I was wrong.

Bob: I understand that you are celebrating your 43rd wedding anniversary tomorrow.

Ray: Yes we are. Actually, it is a celebration of 43 one-year contracts.

Bob: My waist size is the same as when I got married.

Ray: So is mine, but now my waist is much lower.

Bob: **Did you enjoy your holiday visit with your kids?**

Ray: **Yes, and I'm worn out losing to my 10 year old granddaughter at the Wii bowling game!**

Bob: **Tonight I am picking up some Chinese take-out food for a romantic dinner at home.**

Ray: **Remember, 'won ton' spelled backwards is 'not now'.**

Bob: Did you enjoy having your son and his family visit you for Thanksgiving?

Ray: We did. Unfortunately, our son is becoming more like me, however our grandchildren are perfect.

Bob: Do you have any advice for me as a new retiree?

Ray: When someone offers you a breath mint, I would take it.

Bob: Your eyes look bloodshot. Did you have a lot to drink last night?

Ray: No, but your eyes look glazed. Did you eat too many donuts for breakfast?

Betsy: I understand your granddaughter had a vision problem during her Easter weekend visit.

Fred: She was OK, her grandmother just tied her pony tail too tight.

Bob: What do you think of your new doctor?

Ray: I like him. He said I should not exercise until I am in better shape!

Bob: **Congratulations, I understand that your son got engaged over the holidays.**

Ray: **Thanks. I always hoped our kids would get married, now, I hope they stay married.**

Bob: Is there a solution to placing caps on awards for malpractice suits?

Ray: There's a rumor that doctors may stop doing elective surgeries on attorneys.

Bob: My aging process started when I began wearing reading glasses.

Ray: I started to feel older when my hair abandoned ship.

Bob: I learned a lot when I attended the "Earth Day" Seminar this week.

Ray: What would you do if you see an endangered animal eating an endangered plant?

Bob: Since retiring, I understand that you are doing some serious cooking. Would you know the difference between spaghetti and pasta?

Ray: Yes. Eight dollars a pound.

Carolyn: **Are you selling your house?**

Fred: **No. A few clever friends put a sign in my front yard that said, "For Sale by Neighbors".**

Bob: **Did I tell you that before retiring, I spent some time as a "genealogist"?**

Ray: **That profession always confuses me. Does that mean you were a woman's doctor or that you studied rocks?**

Bob: **The fireflies are out in time for tomorrow's first day of summer.**

Ray: **My grandson thinks fireflies are really mosquitoes with flashlights!**

Bob: I understand that your next door neighbors are not getting a divorce.

Ray: Right, neither one wanted custody of the kids.

Bob: This Saturday is the one-year anniversary of "Retired in Williamsburg". Highlights of our debates included what is a Hokie, and Bill Clinton's lack of character.

Ray: As Jerry Seinfeld would say, 'This is a cartoon about nothing'.

Bob: **I heard you are attending a combination golf and self help seminar in Florida to get a grip on your golf game.**

Ray: **I'm taking classes at the brand new "Tiger Woods Anger Management and Driving Academy".**

Bob: Since you retired, are you having problems with short term memory storage?

Ray: Storing memory is not a problem, retrieving it is the problem.

Anita: I read that to prevent identity theft, you should not carry your Social Security number with you.

Rocky: That's a problem. The bureaucratic wizards at Medicare Health Insurance have actually printed my Social Security number on my Medicare Card. No joke!

Bob: I don't look forward to the upcoming holiday parties where I am surrounded by egotists always bragging about themselves.

Ray: There is one advantage, egotists don't talk about other people.

Bob: Now that you are retired, are you sleeping more soundly?

Ray: Yes, but usually at 2:00 in the afternoon.

Bob: **I really enjoyed meeting your 'polite' grandson during his holiday visit.**

Ray: **Thanks, but our daughter describes him as a "house devil and a street angel".**

Bob: Have you finished preparing your income taxes?

Ray: Not yet. I am trying to decide if I should make 3 or 4 honest mistakes on my return!

Bob: A sales rep at ACE Hardware recommended that I subscribe to Popular Mechanics to assist me with my do-it-yourself projects.

Ray: Great idea! I understand it is printed for the mechanically declined.

Sally: **Today is my demanding mother-in-law's birthday and for a gift she has asked for something unusual from the florist.**

Bob: **Send her a Kudzu plant.**

Bob: **Before this holiday season I treated my body as a temple. Now it has become an amusement park.**

Ray: **I am also struggling from what I call the 'wrath of grapes'.**

Bob: **Since retiring, are you assisting your wife with any household chores?**

Ray: **I guess so...the new rule is, "the last one out of bed, has to make it!"**

Bob: Today we are celebrating our 50th wedding anniversary.

Ray: Congratulations. You know, that's equivalent to 350 husband years!

Ray: Did I tell you that my wife is recovering from plastic surgery?

Bob: What was the procedure?

Ray: I cut up her VISA credit card.

Bob: Don't forget, the dress code for tonight's neighborhood party is semi-formal attire.

Ray: That means 'tied shoes'.

Bob: **Did you enjoy your 50th High School reunion?**

Ray: **Yes. But when I arrived at the party, I thought I was joining the parents of the students from my class.**

Bob: **We must remember to continue to support charities as well as our church during this economic downturn.**

Ray: **I agree. I was reminded of our annual pledge last Sunday when our minister gave the sermon on the 'amount'.**

Bob: What do think about the new "green" environmental program that is pushing Reduce, Reuse and Recycle?

Ray: I support it. In fact, this weekend I am sending my wife down to the Virgin Islands to be recycled!

Betty: I understand that your wife just resigned from our health club.

Fred: Yes. By the time she got into her leotard for the last workout, the class was over, so she quit.

Bob: **Did you like Sunday's sermon?**

Ray: **Excellent! It had a good beginning, a good ending, and they were both close together.**

Bob: Now that I am retired, I have the sense that five dollars doesn't buy what it used to buy.

Ray: Actually, the $5 bill will soon be a "coupon" for a gallon of gas!

Bob: **Don't forget, Valentine's Day is eight days from today. By the way, what is your wife's favorite flower?**

Ray: **I think it's Gold Medal All-Purpose.**

CHAPTER 2

. . .

National Politics

Bob: Since our President and Governor have term limits, I think the same should apply to members of Congress.

Ray: The expensive Health Care Reform Bill has passed so the elections on November 2 could be the equivalent of term limits!

Jane: **President's Day is on Monday. Did you know that as President, you must be a 'natural' born citizen?**

Fred: **Ooops, that's a problem for President Obama, since he was delivered by C-section.**

Bob: I wonder if President Obama is pleased with his success in implementing 'change'?

Ray: I am. With new governors in Virginia and New Jersey, and now a new senator in Massachusetts, I can't wait for his next change!

Bob: I voted for President Obama and his promise of change. He said there would be transparency, accountability and job growth . What happened?

Ray: Sounds like 'bait and switch' to me.

Bob: The fees and taxes for the proposed Health Care Legislation will start in 2010, but most of the benefits don't begin until 2014.

Ray: That's because Sen. Reid and Speaker Pelosi attended the 'Bernie Madoff School of Accounting'.

Bob: What does Nancy Pelosi and the fifth largest city in Montana have in common?

Ray: They are both Beautes!

Bob: What do you think is the world's shortest book?

Ray: It's either "The Complete Knowledge of Universal Health Care", by Nancy Pelosi, or, the "Amish Phone Directory".

Bob: By winning the Nobel Peace Prize, President Obama is now in an elite group that includes Mother Theresa and Nelson Mandela.

Ray: Yes, but in President Obama's case, it's like winning an Oscar before the film is made.

Bob: I think you should appreciate the value of the "Public Option" in the proposed Health Care Plan.

Ray: Listen; I was born at night, but not last night!

Marsha: **Looking at our election results, I guess Virginia swing voters are not supporting President Obama and his agenda for "change".**

Tom: **Remember, the only one who likes "change" is a baby with a full diaper!**

Bob: **I can't believe that seven Senators voted this week to continue federal funding for ACORN. They must be suffering from temporary insanity!**

Ray: **I am not sure about the temporary part.**

Bob: What do you mean when you say that we both suffer from "confirmation bias"?

Ray: It's when we concentrate on evidence that supports what we already believe. For example, you watch MSNBC and I watch Fox News!

Becky: Why are you so concerned about President Obama's health?

Gary: Because the next in line to replace him are V.P. Biden, Speaker Pelosi, and Senator Byrd. Yikes!!!

Bob: **Why do you think Thomas Jefferson would object to the cost of President Obama's health care plan?**

Ray: **As Jefferson said, "It is incumbent on every generation to pay it's own debts as it goes".**

Bob: I heard that President Obama's teleprompters are being recalled.

Ray: Like a Toyota, it could explain his rapid acceleration spending problems!

Bob: **Some people think you have become trite with your continuing jab's at our president.**

Ray: **Some people need more fiber!**

Bob: Even as supporter of President Obama, I am concerned with the cost of his new Health Care Plan.

Ray: It will be paid by grandchildren you haven't even met.

Nicole: **Doesn't light travel faster then sound?**

Rick: **Yes, that's why some politicians appear bright until you hear them speak!**

Bob: I am taking my grandchildren to Washington on Monday to attend the annual White House Easter Egg Hunt.

Ray: My father would say that before leaving for Washington, you should sew up your pockets.

Bob: **The Obama administration has made living in Northern Virginia very exciting for my son.**

Ray: **He now lives in what I call "occupied" Virginia!**

Bob: Now that Hillary is our Secretary of State, I understand Bill will visit foreign countries with her.

Ray: Yes. She will ask for support to fight terrorism while he asks for money for the 'fiction section' of his Presidential Library.

Bob: With our growing national debt, I wonder what comes after trillion?

Ray: I'm not sure, but I think President Obama knows.

Bob: In the spirit of the holiday season, you Should stop picking on Bill Clinton.

Ray: O.K. But does Bill really think the Seventh Commandment is 'thou shalt not admit adultery'?

Bob: I am in a state of shocked disbelief. My retirement account has really been under attack.

Ray: I think the battle was actually started by the new Weapons of Mass Destruction, Fannie Mae and Freddie Mac!

Diane: **How can I increase my husband John's heart rate?**

Fred: **Tell him you are voting for Sen. Obama.**

Bob: I applaud President Obama for selecting three of your Republicans as Cabinet Secretaries.

Ray: It's because they know how to fill out their income tax returns without making mistakes!

Bob: I can't remember the first names of the couple who entered the White House last year without credentials.

Ray: Michelle and Barack.

Bob: **When you were working, if you made the mistakes that Congress made trying to pass the financial Bailout Bill, what would have happened to you?**

Ray: **I probably would have been promoted to another Division in my company.**

Bob: I heard that Hillary has finally decided to end her campaign.

Ray: That surprised me. I started to doze before her speech on Tuesday night, and when I woke up during the speech, I thought she had won the nomination!

Barbara: Can you tell the difference between Gov. Sarah Palin and Tina Fey of TV's Saturday Night Live.

Bill: I think Gov. Palin winks with her right eye and Tina Fey winks with her left eye!

Bob: Why are you so suspicious about the Government's proposed Universal Health Care Program?

Ray: The President and Congress are curiously exempt from the Program. If it's good for us, why not for them?

Gerry: I voted for Barack Obama because I wanted to see change and an end to the Clinton agenda.

Ed: Nice try. The Clintons are now on a rebound and their retreads are being appointed by President Obama. In fact, Bill is so popular, he may start dating again.

Bob: I wonder if these government bailouts of large financial institutions are really necessary?

Ray: Reminds me of my wife's checking account since we retired. It is never overdrawn, it's just underdeposited.

Bob: **Is there a solution to stopping birds from hitting an airplane during take off.**

Ray: **How about painting a picture of Nancy Pelosi on the nose of the plane.**

Bob: Why is V.P. Biden attending today's Congressional Black Caucus fundraiser in Williamsburg rather then President Obama?

Ray: The Kingsmill Resort teleprompter is broken.

Bob: **I heard you received a letter from the IRS.**

Ray: **Yes, they were upset that I listed President Obama's "Stimulus Plan" as a dependent on my tax return.**

CHAPTER 3

. . .

Virginia Politics

Bob: **President Obama finally approved drilling for gas in the large reserves off the Virginia coast.**

Ray: **I understand there is as much gas off shore as in the Virginia House and Senate.**

Bob: I have not heard much lately about our part-time Governor.

Ray: Winston Churchill might comment that Gov. Kaine's success is going from failure to failure without loss of enthusiasm.

Bob: **You should stop picking on my fellow Democrat, Gov. Kaine. He tries very hard and is a modest guy.**

Ray: **Yes, our Gov. is very trying and as Winston Churchill might say, "He has much to be modest about"!**

Bob: **I am still disappointed that President-Elect Obama did not select Gov. Kaine for his cabinet?**

Ray: **Gov. Kaine reminds me of a quip by my old friend Walter Kerr, "He has delusions of adequacy."**

Bob: **Remember, we vote for a new Governor on Tuesday. I will miss Governor Kaine. Doesn't he remind you of Truman?**

Ray: **Yes, Truman Capote.**

Bob: **I see that President-Elect Obama finally gave Governor Kaine a job, Chairman of the Democratic National Committee.**

Ray: **With any luck, he can do to the Democratic Party what he did to the highway program in Virginia.**

Bob: Remind me, what are the 3 things you don't want to see being made?

Ray: Politics, Sausage, and Tim Kaine's list of accomplishments as Governor.

Bob: Now that I am a resident of Virginia, I understand that on Tuesday I can vote in either the Democrat "or" Republican Primary.

Ray: It is confusing. I am trying to decide if I want to vote for Obama to knock out Clinton, "or" vote for Huckabee to knock out McCain. It is great to have choices!

Bob: Do you know who actually designed Confusion Corner in Williamsburg?

Ray: I think it was either Benedict Arnold, or the Virginia General Assembly.

Bob: Let's review Tim Kaine's accomplishments as Governor of our Commonwealth.

Ray: ....The silence is deafening!

Bob: Gov. Kaine is trying to look and sound like a fiscal moderate whenever he presents his new Transportation Funding Fix.

Ray: Yes, but I still think he is wearing "tax collector" underwear!

Bob: **I retired from Ohio and I know that a Buckeye is a hairless useless nut. But what is a Hokie?**

Ray: **Same thing.**

Bob: After your comment last Saturday about a Hokie being a hairless, useless nut, I really think you should apologize to the Virginia Tech Alumni.

Ray: I'd rather have a root canal!

Bob: **What about our General Assembly's attempts to impose an additional Grantor's Tax on "house" sales to fund local "road" improvements?**

Ray: **I wish they could see John Adams in the current HBO Series when he says: "It's not that I am against taxes, I am against the way they are imposed". There is a difference.**

Bob: **Did you hear that VDOT successfully tested the Hurricane Gates on I-64 last Sunday morning?**

Ray: **Yes. Now that they work, VDOT will probably install Toll Booths at the gates to pay for road repairs!**

Bob: **I understand that this miserable smoke is coming from fires down in North Carolina.**

Ray: **Oh, I thought the smoke was coming out of Gov. Kaine's ears due to his inability to develop a successful Transportation Bill.**

Bob: I heard you might be moving to Charlottesville.

Ray: My cardiologist thinks I will live longer if I can avoid the excitement of a winning college football program.

CHAPTER 4

. . .

Retirees in Williamsburg

Bob: **Do you know the average age of drivers in Williamsburg?**

Ray: **No, but if a driver has their left signal light flashing, don't assume they will be making a left turn.**

Bob: **As a conservative who moved from James City County into Williamsburg, what are your feelings about the politics here in the City?**

Ray: **I'm very lonely.**

Bob: How is this economic downturn affecting your son who lives in Northern Virginia?

Ray: Well, he is now living in Williamsburg and has two new roommates, his mother and me.

Bob: **Early this morning a cat gave birth to 5 kittens during the Farmer's Market on Duke of Gloucester Street.**

Ray: **Yes, and she was given a ticket for littering!**

Bob: **Do you think Williamsburg restaurants will ever offer valet parking?**

Ray: **I hope so. Valets don't forget where they parked your car.**

Bob: **Traffic on Jamestown Road was stopped this morning as two Canada Geese and their little goslings were crossing the road. Did you know that these geese mate for life?**

Ray: **Yes. That's because they all look alike, so it really doesn't make any difference.**

Bob: **Seriously, what is the best solution for the problem of deer eating our plants?**

Ray: **Alaska Governor Sarah Palin and her recipe for venison sausage.**

Bob: This has been the worst year for deer eating my flowers and shrubs. I wonder where I can go to read about the plants that deer avoid.

Ray: Try the Barnes & Noble Bookstore, Fiction Section.

Bob: With possible tax increases, higher inflation, and escalating health care costs, what concerns you most about this year?

Ray: Right now, ticks and deer!

Bob: **You know, with all the horse droppings on D.O.G. Street, you and I could package and sell the stuff as fertilizer.**

Ray: **Great idea. I'll handle sales.**

Bob: How are you getting along with your new son-in-law from Smithfield?

Ray: The relationship was going well until last night. He almost had a heart attack when I mentioned "reverse mortgages".

Bob: **Are you worried about the CEO of InBev selling Anheuser-Busch assets to pay off debt.**

Ray: **Yes I am. He reminds me of the warning on my car's rear view mirror: "Objects in mirror may be closer than they appear".**

Bob: Smithfield folks claim that they have more original historical buildings then we do, and they refer to us as being from Billysburg!

Ray: I'm sending them some cheddar cheese on the 5:00 pm Ferry to go with their whine.

Bob: **Are you OK with your William and Mary grandson living in a dorm rather than your home?**

Ray: **I think he is happier there. Remember, if you rearrange the letters in 'dormitory', it spells 'dirty room'.**

Bob: The Gazette has added color to some of their cartoons. Do you think that after being here for more than two years, we might be in color?

Ray: That would be like putting a $4 collar on a $2 dog.

Bob: With President Gene Nichol's resignation this week, it is a sad day for William and Mary.

Ray: I agree. But Gene's actions while President reminded me of one of my Dad's favorite expressions; "Don't worry about the horse going blind, just load the wagon".

Jane: **Get ready, this is the start of the important tourist 'Season' for Williamsburg.**

John: **Yes. You can count them but you can't shoot them.**

Bob: **Getting old is scary when you start making the same noises as your coffee maker.**

Ray: **I know what you mean. With the holidays coming up, half the stuff in my shopping cart at the food market says, 'For Fast Relief'.**

Bob: After "InBev" from Belgium buys Anheuser-Busch, I will not drink beer made by a foreign brewing company!

Ray: Well you can't switch to Miller or Coors since South African and Canadian companies own them. How about a nice California chardonnay?

Bob: **As elected JCC supervisors, why would they abstain from voting on the 2009 Budget Proposal when they clearly oppose the budget?**

Ray: **I live in the city, but it must be the politically correct thing to do out in the County.**

Bob: Retirement life in Williamsburg really seems to be agreeing with you.

Ray: If it gets any better, I will have to be two people.

Bob: **I just heard that you are now attending Bruton Parish Church. I thought you were an atheist.**

Ray: **I was. I gave it up…not enough holidays.**

Bob: Yesterday I used my C.W. Good Neighbor Pass and toured the Colonial Jail.

Ray: Great, I understand that is was Williamsburg's first gated community.

Chiles: **Do you think William and Mary will select the "Mighty Wren" as their mascot?**

Fred: **I hope so. Wrens eat Spiders!**

Bob: **Have you completed your volunteer form for the Ladies Michelob Open at Kings Mill?**

Ray: **Yes. In the block where it asks who to contact in the event of an emergency, I put "a good Doctor".**

Bob: Any new business ideas now that you are retired?

Ray: Yes. To improve the service in restaurants in Williamsburg, I am selling Tee shirts that say, "I am not a Tourist, I live here."

Bob: Are you keeping busy on weekends?

Ray: Yes, I started a new business, to allow visitors to rent a dog on Saturdays while they shop at the Farmer's Market on DOG Street.

Bob: **Are you enjoying your volunteer job as a guide at Colonial Williamsburg?**

Ray: **Yes, especially some of the questions. Yesterday I was asked, "Why were all the Revolutionary battles fought in National Parks?"**

Bob: **The William and Mary Sex Worker's Art Show continues to have mixed support for it's appearance next month.**

Ray: **I understand that Tim Kaine, Chairman of the Democratic National Committee and our part-time Governor, supports the Show as a "stimulus" package for the College.**

Bob: What's new?

Ray: I finally told my wife that I was having an affair. She asked me if the Williamsburg Lodge was catering it.

Bob: **Was the design of the parking lot at the Monticello Post Office your last architect's job?**

Ray: **No. Actually, before I retired, my last job was the design of the parking lot at New Town.**

Bob: Why did you retire in Williamsburg?

Ray: Usually when you move to a new city, you find that 25% of the guys are dummies. In Williamsburg, it is only 10%.

Bob: **With state funding for William & Mary below 15%, it appears that the College is no longer state "supported", but state affiliated.**

Ray: **I think William & Mary is really state "located".**

Bob: **I have not heard much lately about the William and Mary Sex Workers Art Show. Are you going?**

Ray: **I don't think so. I heard the actresses' cologne is so powerful that it will knock the shine off your shoes!**

Bob: **Anything new on the selection of a President for William & Mary.**

Ray: **I did hear that the supporters of the annual campus Sex Show are pulling for New York's Governor Eliot Spitzer.**

Bob: **Did you hear the rumor that William & Mary is moving the President's house before the Board of Visitors appoints a new President.**

Ray: **Yes, apparently the house is too close to Confusion Corner.**

Bob: I was very surprised with Gene Nichol's behavior after the Board of Visitors decided not to renew his contract. Sometimes he reminds me of an actor who should be on a stage.

Ray: I agree. The next one to North Carolina leaves in an hour!

Bob: I told my wife to pull the plug if I ever become dependant on a machine and fluids from a bottle.

Ray: Careful, she may unplug your computer and throw out your wine.

Bob: I'm bored with retirement and wondering if I can make some money working part time at Harris Teeter.

Fred: If they pay you what you are worth, they will be violating the Minimum Wage Law.

Made in the USA
Charleston, SC
11 June 2010